Basic Guide to Social Media Marketing

Nishant Baxi

pencil

ISBN 978-93-5883-080-4
© Nishant Baxi 2023

Published in India 2023 by Pencil

A brand of
One Point Six Technologies Pvt. Ltd.
Unit no. 26, Ground Floor, Building A1,
Wadala Truck Terminal Road,
Near Post Office, Antop Hill, Mumbai - 400037
E connect@thepencilapp.com
W www.thepencilapp.com

DISCLAIMER: *The opinions expressed in this book are those of the authors and do not purport to reflect the views of the Publisher.*

Author biography

I am an experienced content creator and digital/social media marketing professional with a demonstrated history of working in the publishing industry. I am skilled in E-Learning, Market Research, Online Advertising, Management, and Business Development, Content Development.

CONTENTS

Introduction

Definition of Social Media Marketing

With the explosion of digital communication, businesses have increasingly turned to social media platforms to market their products and services. This utilization of social platforms to drive consumer engagement and stimulate interest in products, services, or ideas is known today as social media marketing (SMM).

SMM is a type of internet marketing that exploits various social media networks to achieve marketing communication and branding goals. It predominantly involves content creation and sharing on different social media channels to accomplish marketing and branding objectives (Investopedia, 2020). In simpler terms, it leverages social media platforms like Facebook, Twitter, Instagram, and LinkedIn to promote a product or service and engage with a brand's audience.

SMM allows businesses to reach potential customers faster than traditional marketing. Since social media sites allow people to interact with one another, they serve as a practical tool for companies to communicate directly with their customers (Hootsuite, 2017). Furthermore, businesses can gain invaluable insights from these social interactions about their audiences' opinions, behavioral tendencies, and preferences.

The tactics used in SMM are diverse. Primarily, companies use it to share content, images, videos, and links to promote their products or services and generate user engagement. Some of the strategies include posting text and image updates, videos, and other content that drives an engaged audience, as well as paid social media advertising (SproutSocial, 2019).

It's essential to understand that not all social media platforms are applicable for every business type. Hence, identifying the most suitable platform is of utmost importance. Businesses need to ascertain where their target audience spends most of their time and focus their marketing efforts on those platforms (Buffer, 2018). For instance, a fashion brand might find Instagram more beneficial than LinkedIn.

One of the major benefits of implementing an SMM strategy is that it helps increase brand awareness. By regularly interacting with their audience, businesses can build their reputation and establish a wider customer base. Furthermore, it can improve brand loyalty, as customers appreciate knowing that if they post comments on your pages, they will receive personalized responses (Forbes, 2018).

In conclusion, social media marketing has become an integral part of every marketing strategy. The digital age has made it essential for businesses to have a social presence to succeed in the marketplace. Its potential to interact directly with customers and the opportunity to create a more personalized experience makes SMM a bright implement in the marketing toolbox.

Relevance of Social Media Marketing in Today's Business Landscape

In the current digitalized era, the significance of social media marketing cannot be understated. An immeasurable array of businesses has recognized its efficacy and adopted it into their marketing strategies (Patel, 2020). Considering its reachability, cost-effectiveness, and instant communication, the platform constitutes an indispensable tool in contemporary commerce.

A report by Datareportal (2021) articulated that over 4.20 billion people globally are active social media users, signifying a penetration rate of 53.6%. Therefore, the use of social media has the potential for businesses to reach out to a huge percentage of potential customers effectively. As such, social media marketing offers businesses an opportunity to reach a broad audience without geographic constraints.

In addition to wider outreach, social media marketing also provides a cost-effective marketing strategy. Traditional forms of marketing, such as TV commercials, print media, and billboard ads, are often costly, especially for smaller businesses. Social media marketing, on the other hand, may only require business owners to invest in creating high-quality content and dedicate time for interaction with their audience (Newberry, 2021). This cost-effective nature of social media marketing has proved instrumental, especially in the era where frugal budgets have become a necessity.

Arguably, one of the most compelling reasons to adopt social media marketing is its facilitation of instant communication. Through such platforms, businesses can interact with their customers in real-time, increasing engagement and building trust. Providing timely responses and viable solutions augments customer satisfaction, thus fostering customer loyalty (Miller, 2020).

Analytical power is another relevant factor of social media marketing. Platforms such as Facebook, LinkedIn, and Instagram integrate analytical tools that help businesses to track the success of their campaigns. This real-time feedback is essential for the business to adjust its strategy promptly if a campaign is not resonating well with the audience (Agius, 2021).

Moreover, social media marketing plays a pivotal role in enhancing brand visibility and reputation. Regular updates about products and services, policy changes, or philanthropic ventures can keep audiences informed and engaged. Besides, sharing content related to business values and social responsibilities can help in building a positive brand perception (Brenner, 2020).

In conclusion, the relevance of social media marketing in contemporary business is incontrovertible. The vast potential audience reaches cost-effectiveness, interactive communication, analytical capabilities, and brand reputation enhancement rendering this tool a must for businesses of any size or type. It's high time businesses that haven't yet incorporated it into their strategies reconsider their marketing approach.

Purpose of the eBook

In today's digital era, social media marketing has become an integral part of most successful businesses' strategies. Hootsuite (2020), reveals that approximately 3.8 billion people worldwide use social media, thus providing businesses a vast audience to target and interact with. Among the many marketing methods available, social media marketing undeniably stands out as an effective and exceptionally lucrative tool.

Social media marketing, as per Sharma (2020), is the use of social media platforms to promote a product or service. It involves creating content that is tailored to the specific context of each platform, to drive user engagement and sharing. These platforms, which include Facebook, Instagram, Twitter, LinkedIn, Pinterest, YouTube, and Snapchat, provide businesses with a way to reach new customers, engage with existing ones, and promote their desired culture, mission, or tone.

One of the primary purposes of social media marketing is brand recognition. Creating social media profiles offers a chance to broaden your business visibility. By applying a robust social media strategy, your brand can significantly increase its reach. Every share, like, or comment can lead your company to a new network of individuals which can eventually lead to potential customers or clients.

Another crucial purpose is improving business customer service. Customers expect businesses to be available and responsive on social media for inquiries and feedback. For instance, Twitter has become a popular customer service tool with 85% of SMB Twitter users saying they feel more connected to businesses after becoming their followers (Twitter, 2019).

Social media marketing also allows for better market insight. Through interaction with customers on social media, businesses can understand what consumers need and like. It opens up a platform for surveys and feedback which will lead your business to develop more strategic marketing plans.

Lastly, one of the main benefits of social media marketing is cost-effectiveness. Setting up profiles on social media platforms is free, and if you decide to go for paid advertising, you can start small to see what works best. Even paid social media advertisements offer a higher return on investment than traditional advertising.

Undoubtedly, the purposes of social media marketing reach beyond mere advertising. It is a powerful tool for businesses to establish their brand, connect with their audience, understand the market, and eventually boost sales.

Therefore, mastering social media marketing is an invaluable skill in this increasingly digital business environment. By understanding its purpose and learning effective strategies, businesses can build stronger relationships with their audience, and in turn, stride toward sustained success.

Understanding Social Media

Overview of Different Social Media Platforms

Introduction

In the digital era, the essential requirements for personal and business growth incorporate the appropriate and effective use of multiple social media platforms. Each platform attracts unique demographics and contains distinct features, driving various engagement types (Smith, 2021). It becomes necessary to understand the differences between these platforms, their usage, effectiveness, and their position in the social media landscape.

Facebook

Facebook, founded in 2004, has grown substantially impacting the social media ecosystem. With over 2.8 billion monthly users approving its mammoth presence (Statista, 2022), it predates and outstrips most social networks. This platform allows users to share text-based updates, photos, and videos besides offering a myriad of other features. Its demographic is extensive; however, it's popular among adults aged 25-34 years(Statista, 2022).

Instagram

Owned by Facebook, Instagram launched in 2010 has gained considerable recognition for its image-based sharing feature. It provides various secondary features such as stories, reels, and IGTV. Instagram has a user base leaning towards individuals aged 18-34 years, predominantly female (Statista, 2022). It caters to an environment submerged in visual aesthetics making it ideal for businesses that work well with presentations capable of visual captivation.

Twitter

Contrasting the image-centric Instagram, Twitter emphasizes text-based posts (tweets) and real-time information. Launched in 2006, Twitter serves as a haven for trending topics and often surpasses other platforms in real-time news discussions. The user base tends to be younger (18-29 years), including journalists, celebrities, and politicians who commonly utilize the 280-character limit post (Smith, 2021).

LinkedIn

Originating as a professional social networking platform in 2003, LinkedIn stands apart for its focus on job-related content, professional networking, industry discussions, and job postings. Aimed at professionals across industries, it becomes essential for Business-to-Business (B2B) marketing (Statista, 2022).

YouTube

In the video-sharing landscape, YouTube (born 2005) dominates. This platform allows users to upload, share, and view video content. Businesses can utilize it for video tutorials, product launches, vlogs, and more. YouTube spans a significant demographic range, but its key users are aged between 15-25 years (Statista, 2022).

Pinterest

Launched in 2010, Pinterest behaves as a search engine for ideas. Users 'pin' images, which represent interests or ideas to 'boards' for future reference. It is primarily utilized by females (77% of its users) and can be an effective platform for brands and products appealing to this particular demographic(Smith, 2021).

Conclusion

While all social media platforms offer opportunities for engagement and community building, discerning the nuances of each can optimize the benefits. Businesses and individuals alike must evaluate the strengths and weaknesses of these platforms to formulate an effective social media strategy.

Key Characteristics of Different Social Media Platforms

In the digital age, social media platforms are a crucial part of everyday life, shaping how we communicate, stay informed, and engage with the world. The marketplace of social media platforms is vast and diverse; each platform possesses distinctive attributes that appeal to different demographics and are used for various purposes. Understanding these key characteristics of each platform can help users and businesses alike to leverage them effectively (Rossi, 2021).

Facebook is the kingpin of social media, boasting a broad demographic and an immense user base. Its key attribute lies in its versatility; it is a powerful platform for sharing wide-ranging content types, including text, photos, and videos. Facebook also offers several tools for businesses, such as targeted advertising and analytics (Associated Press, 2021).

Twitter's unique characteristic lies in its brevity and immediacy. It is a real-time information network, perfect for news updates. With a 280-character limit, Twitter focuses on succinct communication making it an ideal platform for brand announcements and customer service (Yusuf, 2021).

Instagram is a highly visual platform centering on photo and video sharing. It is an essential tool for influencer marketing due to its highly engaged young demographic. Instagram offers a wide range of visual content, including photos, Stories, IGTV, and Reels (Manwani, 2021).

LinkedIn is a professional networking platform designed for business-to-business communication. It is a prime platform for recruiting, professional growth, and career networking and is increasingly becoming a hub for thought leadership (Sethi, 2021).

Pinterest is the go-to platform for visual discovery and planning. Users "pin" images linked to webpages onto themed boards. Primarily used for planning projects and events, or finding inspiration, Pinterest is popular among a female demographic interested in DIY, home decor, recipes, and fashion (Pinterest, 2021).

Finally, TikTok, a newcomer to the scene, focuses on short, amusing video clips. It has reached mass popularity among younger users. With its viral challenges and dance crazes, TikTok provides engaging user-generated content and offers significant opportunities for businesses to gain exposure (Zhang, 2021).

Each social media platform has unique attributes that differentiate them and satisfy different needs. Understanding the nature of these platforms can support personal and business communication, allowing us to navigate the dynamic landscape of digital networking.

Benefits of Using Social Media for Marketing

In late modernity, social media is no longer simply a recreational tool utilized for individual networking; it has, in essence, become an instrumental component within the canvas of contemporary marketing strategies. With an incredible 3.6 billion users of social media worldwide as of 2020 and projections of this number swelling to 4.41 billion by 2025, marketers have increasingly recognized the colossal potential of these platforms in creating brand visibility, engagement, and conversion (Kemp, 2021). The benefits of implementing social media within marketing strategies are indeed vast.

Foremostly, social media platforms have evolved as channels providing unprecedented accessibility to a global audience base. This global reach fosters brand exposure and visibility, thus providing enterprises with the opportunity to extend their services and products to a broader prospective consumer population. Additionally, nuanced, geographical, socio-economic, and demographic data provided by these platforms allow marketers to cater to specific audience demographics, thereby enhancing efficiency in ad spending (Kim, 2018).

Overview of Different Social Media Platforms

Introduction

In the digital era, the essential requirements for personal and business growth incorporate the appropriate and effective use of multiple social media platforms. Each platform attracts unique demographics and contains distinct features, driving various engagement types (Smith, 2021). It becomes necessary to understand the differences between these platforms, their usage, effectiveness, and their position in the social media landscape.

Facebook

Facebook, founded in 2004, has grown substantially impacting the social media ecosystem. With over 2.8 billion monthly users approving its mammoth presence (Statista, 2022), it predates and outstrips most social networks. This platform allows users to share text-based updates, photos, and videos besides offering a myriad of other features. Its demographic is extensive; however, it's popular among adults aged 25-34 years(Statista, 2022).

Instagram

Owned by Facebook, Instagram launched in 2010 has gained considerable recognition for its image-based sharing feature. It provides various secondary features such as stories, reels, and IGTV. Instagram has a user base leaning towards individuals aged 18-34 years, predominantly female (Statista, 2022). It caters to an environment submerged in visual aesthetics making it ideal for businesses that work well with presentations capable of visual captivation.

Twitter

Contrasting the image-centric Instagram, Twitter emphasizes text-based posts (tweets) and real-time information. Launched in 2006, Twitter serves as a haven for trending topics and often surpasses other platforms in real-time news discussions. The user base tends to be younger (18-29 years), including journalists, celebrities, and politicians who commonly utilize the 280-character limit post (Smith, 2021).

LinkedIn

Originating as a professional social networking platform in 2003, LinkedIn stands apart for its focus on job-related content, professional networking, industry discussions, and job postings. Aimed at professionals across industries, it becomes essential for Business-to-Business (B2B) marketing (Statista, 2022).

YouTube

In the video-sharing landscape, YouTube (born 2005) dominates. This platform allows users to upload, share, and view video content. Businesses can utilize it for video tutorials, product launches, vlogs, and more. YouTube spans a significant demographic range, but its key users are aged between 15-25 years (Statista, 2022).

Pinterest

Launched in 2010, Pinterest behaves as a search engine for ideas. Users 'pin' images, which represent interests or ideas to 'boards' for future reference. It is primarily utilized by females (77% of its users) and can be an effective platform for brands and products appealing to this particular demographic(Smith, 2021).

Conclusion

While all social media platforms offer opportunities for engagement and community building, discerning the nuances of each can optimize the benefits. Businesses and individuals alike must evaluate the strengths and weaknesses of these platforms to formulate an effective social media strategy.

Key Characteristics of Different Social Media Platforms

In the digital age, social media platforms are a crucial part of everyday life, shaping how we communicate, stay informed, and engage with the world. The marketplace of social media platforms is vast and diverse; each platform possesses distinctive attributes that appeal to different demographics and are used for various purposes. Understanding these key characteristics of each platform can help users and businesses alike to leverage them effectively (Rossi, 2021).

Facebook is the kingpin of social media, boasting a broad demographic and an immense user base. Its key attribute lies in its versatility; it is a powerful platform for sharing wide-ranging content types, including text, photos, and videos. Facebook also offers several tools for businesses, such as targeted advertising and analytics (Associated Press, 2021).

Twitter's unique characteristic lies in its brevity and immediacy. It is a real-time information network, perfect for news updates. With a 280-character limit, Twitter focuses on succinct communication making it an ideal platform for brand announcements and customer service (Yusuf, 2021).

Instagram is a highly visual platform centering on photo and video sharing. It is an essential tool for influencer marketing due to its highly engaged young demographic. Instagram offers a wide range of visual content, including photos, Stories, IGTV, and Reels (Manwani, 2021).

LinkedIn is a professional networking platform designed for business-to-business communication. It is a prime platform for recruiting, professional growth, and career networking and is increasingly becoming a hub for thought leadership (Sethi, 2021).

Pinterest is the go-to platform for visual discovery and planning. Users "pin" images linked to webpages onto themed boards. Primarily used for planning projects and events, or finding inspiration, Pinterest is popular among a female demographic interested in DIY, home decor, recipes, and fashion (Pinterest, 2021).

Finally, TikTok, a newcomer to the scene, focuses on short, amusing video clips. It has reached mass popularity among younger users. With its viral challenges and dance crazes, TikTok provides engaging user-generated content and offers significant opportunities for businesses to gain exposure (Zhang, 2021).

Each social media platform has unique attributes that differentiate them and satisfy different needs. Understanding the nature of these platforms can support personal and business communication, allowing us to navigate the dynamic landscape of digital networking.

Benefits of Using Social Media for Marketing

In late modernity, social media is no longer simply a recreational tool utilized for individual networking; it has, in essence, become an instrumental component within the canvas of contemporary marketing strategies. With an incredible 3.6 billion users of social media worldwide as of 2020 and projections of this number swelling to 4.41 billion by 2025, marketers have increasingly recognized the colossal potential of these platforms in creating brand visibility, engagement, and conversion (Kemp, 2021). The benefits of implementing social media within marketing strategies are indeed vast.

Foremostly, social media platforms have evolved as channels providing unprecedented accessibility to a global audience base. This global reach fosters brand exposure and visibility, thus providing enterprises with the opportunity to extend their services and products to a broader prospective consumer population. Additionally, nuanced, geographical, socio-economic, and demographic data provided by these platforms allow marketers to cater to specific audience demographics, thereby enhancing efficiency in ad spending (Kim, 2018).

Further, social media, with its interactive features facilitates the creation of a lively, online community where engagement and two-way communication thrive. This mechanism serves not only to reinforce brand-customer relationships but also to provide invaluable consumer behavior insights. By observing user comments, replies, likes, and shares, businesses can tailor their marketing strategies to better meet their audience's needs, wants, and expectations (Tuten & Solomon, 2017).

Moreover, social media acts as an effective customer service tool, providing swift resolution to customer queries and complaints, thereby fostering customer satisfaction and loyalty. Responsiveness, in turn, encourages word-of-mouth referrals, augmenting brand reputation and credibility.

Interestingly, social media also offers cost-effectiveness in advertising. Compared to traditional marketing methods, social media marketing entails meager costs. Many platforms even offer free business accounts, which provide various tools such as analytics, ad creation, and scheduling options. Paid social media ads are also relatively inexpensive and can fit in almost any small or big business's budget.

Finally, the incorporation of social media in marketing strategy significantly boosts website traffic. By sharing useful, intriguing content alongside active website links, chances of converting social media users to website visitors, and potentially customers, escalate. This tactic is wonderfully supported by Search Engine Optimization (SEO) benefits, where consistent social media postings can enhance search engine result rankings, thereby indirectly promoting visibility.

In conclusion, the integration of social media within marketing strategies stands as a powerful leverage tool that can reap significant benefits in brand promotion, audience engagement, and revenue generation.

Fundamentals of Social Media Marketing

Setting up Social Media Profiles

In this digital age, both individuals and businesses need to maintain a solid presence on social media platforms. Social media profiles act as the digital face of a person or a brand, and hence, their setup and maintenance hold paramount importance. This article provides a comprehensive guide on setting up social media profiles to attain an impactful digital persona.

When it comes to setting up a social media profile, the first decision to be made is regarding the platform selection. Commonly used social media platforms include Facebook, Instagram, Twitter, LinkedIn, and Pinterest. You should choose your platforms based on where your potential audience is most likely to engage (Algonquin College, n.d.). After selecting the platform, the next step is creating an account. This usually requires a name, email address, and a password. After this, the journey to setting up a compelling profile begins. Here are some key points to consider:

Profile Picture: Often the first aspect people notice, the profile picture should ideally be a professional photo or a high-quality logo for businesses (Sprout Social, 2020).

Bio/Profile Description: This gives a brief overview of who you are or what your business does. Keep it concise, clear, and compelling.

Contact Information: Ensure that your contact details are accurate and up-to-date. For businesses, providing a website URL is also crucial.

Cover Photo: For platforms such as Facebook and Twitter, the cover photo offers another opportunity to make an impact.

Posting Schedule: Regularly posting content fosters engagement and retention of your audience base.

Even after a successful setup, the optimization of social media profiles should be an ongoing process. Keep updating your profile with notable achievements, recent projects, and a fresh array of engaging content.

Now, moving on to security. It is essential to set a strong, unique password and activate any available security features. Also, privacy settings need to be adjusted based on your comfort and requirements for visibility.

Finally, cross-promotion on different social media platforms is a great way to ensure widespread reach. Promote your Instagram on Twitter, your Twitter on Facebook, and so on to gain maximum visibility.

In conclusion, setting up social media profiles is not just about creating an account; it requires thoughtful planning and regular optimization. With a well-set-up profile, you can leverage the power of social media to amplify your digital presence, engage with your audience, and grow your influence or business.

Content Creation

Social media is a pivotal component of business marketing strategies. In contemporary business environments, being able to create engaging and appealing social media content is indispensable. Indeed, the role that social media content creation plays in keeping one's audience interested and engaged cannot be underestimated. This article seeks to demystify social media content creation and what it entails (1).

Social media content creation primarily involves developing unique content that is engaging to your targeted audience and pertinent to your brand. This also encompasses deciding on the type of content to post, how often to post, and responding to audience feedback. Effective social media content should be visually appealing, compelling, and relevant to your audience. It should also articulate the value of your brand, products, or services, thereby converting followers into customers.

Creating engaging social media content requires a deep understanding of one's target audience and their preferences. This involves identifying your ideal customers, understanding their needs, and tailoring your content to resonate with them. It's paramount to adopt a customer-centric approach while creating your social media content, ensuring your content compellingly answers the question of 'what's in it for me?' from your audience's perspective.

Further, the power of visual appeal in social media content creation cannot be overstated. Visual content, including images, infographics, and videos, has a higher likelihood of capturing your audience's attention than plain text. Therefore, incorporating visuals into your social media content strategy is beneficial for disseminating complex information in a simple, understandable, and memorable manner. Moreover, visual content is statistically proven to increase engagement rates on most platforms (2).

Creating a content calendar for planning when and what to post can save time and help strategize your posts matching different campaigns or promotional periods. Scheduling tools for social media can assist you in managing your content while targeting your messages according to the different time zones of users.

Lastly, analyzing your social media content performance is highly crucial. By employing social media analytics, you can understand better what type of content resonates with your audience, and optimal posting times, and gauge your return on investment. Metrics such as engagement, reach, and conversion rate provide valuable insight into the efficacy of your social media content strategy, enabling necessary adjustments for better performance.

In conclusion, effective social media content creation entails understanding your audience, creating visually appealing and relevant content, utilizing a content calendar, and analyzing your content performance.

Understanding Social Media Algorithm

Social media platforms have become a crucial part of our daily routine. As such, both individuals and corporate entities must understand how these platforms work, particularly their algorithms, to effectively disseminate information and engage with their audience.

Social media algorithms are a series of computations put in place by online platforms to organize, manage, and prioritize content seamlessly. These calculations determine the content that appears on a user's feed based on behavior, interests, connections, and other metrics (Neher, 2013). Understanding these algorithms aids in maximizing the reach and engagement of your content.

The base of these algorithms revolves around relevance. For instance, Facebook's algorithm prioritizes posts from friends and pages a user frequently interacts with. The more the interaction, the more likely related content will be shown on their feed (Kim, 2019). This goes back to the user behavior and tracking metrics the algorithm follows; the more active a user is with specific content, the higher the chances of that content appearing on their timeline.

Instagram also operates on a similar mechanism, focusing on user interests to prioritize the posts seen on the user's feed. The social media platform utilizes machine-learning technology to track the user's likes, shares, and searches. Thus, posts users previously interacted with or searched for will likely surface on their feed (McGovern, 2020).

Twitter's algorithm, on the other hand, offers both chronological and algorithmic timelines for its users. By default, Twitter showcases a mixture of tweets from accounts the user follows based on their interests. However, users still have the option to switch to a chronological timeline.

The YouTube algorithm works differently, focusing on watch time rather than views. It recommends videos based on the length of time users spend watching a certain type of video. This insight is crucial for content creators aiming to increase their viewership (Banker, 2020).

In conclusion, understanding social media algorithms is paramount for effective social media marketing. The algorithms shape the social media environment, personalizing content for each user based on their interests and behaviors. As these computations continue to evolve, it's essential to stay ahead and adapt your content strategy accordingly to maximize reach and engagement.

Building Social Media Presence

Increasingly, businesses are recognizing the immense potential of social media to connect with a diverse, widespread audience. Building a strong social media presence is not a mere luxury but a powerful necessity in today's digital business landscape (Smith, 2020). This article elucidates key steps to effective social media strategy and presence.

The primary step in building strong social media visibility entails understanding the targeted audience. A business should conduct thorough research to comprehend whom it's trying to reach. Understanding the demographic profiles, interests, and online behaviors of the intended audience allows businesses to tailor the content to their preferences (Johnson, 2018). Facebook Audience Insights and Google Analytics are handy tools for demographic analysis.

Secondly, choosing the right platform is integral. Businesses should establish their presence on platforms their targeted audiences mostly use. For instance, brands targeting young adults can capitalize on Instagram or Snapchat, while LinkedIn is apt for B2B companies (Mandler, 2017).

Consistency is another crucial aspect of social media presence. Consistent brand language, aesthetics, and posting schedules establish the reliability and foster the audience's trust. Tools like Buffer and Hootsuite facilitate automating posts and maintaining regular engagement.

Creating engaging content is crucial. Consistently delivering valuable, relatable, and interactive content captivates audiences, prompting them to share, thereby amplifying brand reach and awareness (Barker, 2020). An attractive blend of visuals and text, interactive polls and Q&As, behind-the-scenes content, and user-generated content can facilitate strong audience engagement.

Connecting and interacting with the audience is also

essential. Social media provides businesses with an unparalleled opportunity to humanize their brands, exhibit transparency, and listen to their audiences (Agrawal, 2019). Businesses should routinely respond to comments, direct messages, and audience queries, fostering relationship building.

Lastly, analyzing and refining strategies periodically is fundamental for persistent success. Businesses should regularly measure key performance indicators (KPIs), track audience responses, and assess impacts to adjust and fine-tune their social media strategies.

In conclusion, building a substantial social media presence requires a well-planned and executed strategy that aligns with the business goals. Consistent audience-centric content, selected platforms, engagement, and regular analysis and refinement of strategies cultivate a remarkable social media presence in the digital landscape.

Advanced Social Media Marketing Strategies

Use of Social Media Advertising

In the contemporary digital age, businesses are increasingly adopting social media advertising to reach their target audience more efficiently. This approach has been catalyzed by the ever-growing number of social media users worldwide, which is estimated to reach 3.6 billion in 2020 (Statist, 2020). Consequently, social media platforms offer businesses a fertile ground to grow their brand visibility, foster customer engagement, and ultimately drive sales.

Social media advertising refers to the process of creating content and then effectively employing the purpose-built advertising features of social media platforms such as Facebook, Instagram, LinkedIn, Twitter, and TikTok, among others, to reach specific populations of users (Chaffey et al., 2019). These features include sponsored posts, targeted ads, and stories, which are customized to resonate with specific user interests, demographics, or behavioral trends.

One of the key benefits of social media advertising is its ability to tap into granular audience targeting. For instance, Facebook and Instagram allow advertisers to define their target audience based on demographics, user locations, interests, behaviors, and connections (Stelzner, 2019). This targeted approach helps businesses present their content to the users who are more likely to convert, thereby optimizing the advertisement ROI.

As per Social Media Examiner's annual report, 93% of marketers affirmed the efficacy of social media advertising in driving traffic and generating leads (Stelzner, 2019). This indicates that social media advertising is not only used for branding but also has a strong correlation with bottom-line results. Moreover, marketers can use social media metrics, analytics, and insights to track their advertising performance, gauge customer engagement, and adjust their strategy promptly based on the data.

Furthermore, social media advertising fosters direct interaction and engagement with users. Platforms enable users to share, comment, like, and directly message businesses about the advertised content (Chaffey et al., 2019). This interactive relationship enhances customer loyalty and sentiment toward the brand.

As businesses look to achieve improved marketing results, leveraging social media advertising ought to be a serious consideration. The platforms offer a cost-effective, highly targeted, and user-engaging medium to reach potential customers and thereby bolster strategic growth.

Influencer Marketing

Influencer marketing continues to be a major player in modern marketing strategies, particularly with the continual rise of social media and its inherent interactivity. Organizations are increasingly leveraging the power of influencers to enhance their brand image, spark meaningful conversations, and ultimately drive sales.

In simple terms, influencer marketing refers to a form of the social media marketing that uses endorsements and product mentions from influencers – individuals who possess a dedicated social media following and are viewed as experts within their niche (Freberg, Graham, McGaughey, & Freberg, 2011). Influencers have a unique ability to generate trust and credibility amongst their followers, thus influencing their purchasing decisions by effectively serving as a conduit for brands' marketing messages.

The effectiveness of influencer marketing largely relies on the selection of the right influencer. Research indicates that influencers, who resemble the target audience in terms of age, gender, or lifestyle, tend to have a deeper impact (Lou & Yuan, 2019). Furthermore, influencers with engaged and active followers often yield better marketing results than those with large, passive follower bases.

Businesses considering the use of influencer marketing should align influencer partnerships with their brand message and values to ensure authenticity. Moreover, campaigns should focus on creating compelling and original content that stands out among the cluttered social media landscape.

Understanding the metrics used to determine the success of influencer marketing campaigns is also crucial. Metrics can include the number of likes, shares, comments, clicks, conversions, or overall reach a campaign has achieved (De Veirman, Cauberghe, & Hudders, 2017).

Despite its obvious advantages, influencer marketing does present challenges. Maintaining authenticity can be difficult if influencers are viewed as merely promoting products for compensation. Furthermore, the impact of influencer marketing on return on investment (ROI) is not always immediately apparent, requiring patience and perseverance from marketers.

In conclusion, influencer marketing is an innovative approach to reach modern consumers who increasingly rely on social media for information and inspiration. By strategically leveraging the power of influencers, organizations can deeply connect with their target audience, foster brand engagement, and ultimately drive sales.

Analytics and Performance Monitoring

In today's digital era, social media marketing plays an essential role in reaching out to potential customers and maintaining consistent engagement with existing ones. To make the most effective use of social media platforms for marketing, analytics, and performance monitoring are pivotal. This paper will discuss the importance of social media marketing analytics and performance monitoring.

Social media marketing analytics serve as a quantifiable measure for determining the success of a business's marketing strategies. Organizations use this data to assess the effectiveness of their social media presence and campaigns. Analytics can include metrics such as target audience demographics, peak engagement times, popular post types, and more (Smith, 2020). Leveraging these data points allows businesses to tailor their content and strategies to their audience's preferences, maximizing their marketing efforts' impact.

Furthermore, performance monitoring, another integral aspect of social media marketing, helps companies track the progress of their marketing initiatives on multiple social media platforms. Tools designed for performance monitoring offer comprehensive insights into a campaign's reach, impressions, engagement, click-through rates, and overall return on investment (ROI).

Performance monitoring allows for real-time tracking, offering businesses the agility to modify their approach as necessary swiftly. This capability is invaluable in today's rapidly changing digital sphere, as it ensures businesses remain relevant and competitive. It also promotes a data-driven culture, encouraging organizations to make more educated decisions based on factual data rather than gut feelings or anecdotal experiences (Klein, 2019).

Up-to-date, accurate analytics and performance monitoring can help businesses capitalize on their social media activities. They can understand what content generates the most engagement, determine the most effective strategies for increasing visibility, and assess which platform offers the best return on investment. As social media continues to evolve and businesses continue to leverage these platforms for marketing, these tools' importance will only continue to grow.

In conclusion, the integration of social media marketing analytics and performance monitoring is a powerful combination. It not only enables businesses to optimize their strategies but also delivers insights to drive decision-making processes. Businesses need to utilize these resources to ensure their social media marketing efforts are effectively reaching their target audiences and achieving their goals.

Case Studies

Examples of Successful Social Media Marketing Campaigns

In an era driven by digital media, social media marketing stands as a potent tool for businesses to effectively interact with their audience and promote their brand. Several global brands have efficiently utilized social media platforms to perform groundbreaking marketing campaigns. Let's explore some notable examples of successful social media marketing campaigns.

1. Dove's Real Beauty Sketches Campaign

Arguably one of the most successful social media marketing campaigns to date, Dove's Real Beauty Sketches aimed to redefine beauty standards swept social media off its feet in 2013. It comprised a series of videos where a forensic sketch artist drew women's portraits based on their self-description and then those given by strangers. The campaign resonated with the audience as it portrayed the insecurities that women often encounter concerning their physical appearance (Forbes, 2013).

2. ALS Ice Bucket Challenge

One of the most viral social media marketing campaigns in history can rightly be awarded to the ALS Ice Bucket Challenge. Advocating for amyotrophic lateral sclerosis (ALS), the campaign raised awareness by challenging individuals to dump a bucket of ice on themselves within

24 hours of being nominated or donate to the ALS association. It not only raised approximately $115 million for the cause but also became an international sensation that witnessed participation from celebrities, political figures, and influencers alike (TIME, 2014).

3. Starbucks' Unicorn Frappuccino Campaign

In 2017, Starbucks launched a limited-edition Unicorn Frappuccino. Using the hashtag #UnicornFrappuccino on Instagram, they promoted a vibrant, rainbow-themed beverage that gained massive traction on social media. This engagement was significantly fueled by user-generated content, with consumers posting their images with the unicorn drink. Consequently, the campaign garnered huge attention while promoting their brand (CNBC, 2017).

4. Airbnb's #WeAccept Campaign

Airbnb, to strengthen their policy of non-discrimination, launched the #WeAccept campaign in 2017. The campaign promoted inclusivity and acceptance of all races, religions, genders, and nationalities across its host and guest platform in response to the travel ban imposed by the U.S. administration. A compact video ad was posted on various social media channels, reaching millions of people globally and bolstering Airbnb's commitment to reducing bias (Ad Age, 2017).

5. Spotify's 2018 Goals Campaign

Utilizing the power of humor and user-generated data, Spotify's 2018 Goals campaign stormed the internet. Individual billboards showcased users' quirky playlist names or unexpected music choices from the previous year, thereby turning personal data into an engaging and humorous marketing strategy (Adweek, 2018).

These campaigns are only a handful of examples demonstrating successful social media marketing, each designed with thoughtful planning and execution. By resonating with their target audience and banking on topical and social trends, these brands managed to instigate virality and generate heightened brand visibility.

Developing a Social Media Marketing Plan

In today's digitalized world, social media has become a powerful marketing tool capable of reaching all corners of the earth at a moment's notice. However, for businesses to harness this potential effectively, they need to develop a robust social media marketing plan. This guide will walk you through the fundamental steps necessary to establish a comprehensive social media marketing plan.

The first phase involves setting clear and attainable objectives. Setting objectives translates into having a clear roadmap to gauge performance and drive strategic adjustments (1). Objectives should align with the broader corporate goals and must be specific, measurable, attainable, relevant, and timely (SMART) (2).

Once objectives have been formalized, knowing your target audience is the next crucial step in this plan. An in-depth understanding of who your audience is, what they want, and how they interact on various social media platforms will shape the creation and delivery of your content (1). Demographic data, user behavior insights, and target audience preferences play a significant role in content customization.

Equally important is selecting an appropriate social media platform. The choice of the platform goes hand-in-hand with the nature of the target audience. Businesses need to identify where their audience spends most of their time and focus their efforts there. Different social media platforms attract different user demographics, hence the importance of knowing your audience (3).

The content is the vehicle through which your message is conveyed, so it must be captivating and provide value to the target audience (4). The development of an editorial calendar to organize and schedule content release will ensure consistent delivery, another critical factor in retaining audience interest.

Finally, tracking and adaptation form the last stage of developing a social media marketing plan. Given the dynamic nature of social media, businesses must actively monitor their progress using built-in platform analytics or third-party tools (5). Scrutinizing metrics allows for the identification of strategic shortfalls and opportunities for improvement. To stay competitive, businesses need to adapt their strategies in line with evolving trends and audience preferences.

Implementing a social media marketing plan is not a one-time event. It calls for continuous effort, commitment, and adaptability in response to the ever-changing social media landscape. Following these steps will put businesses on a robust path towards achieving a formidable online presence and gaining a competitive edge in the digital market.

Common Challenges in Social Media Marketing and How to Overcome Them

Social media has progressed from a fringe marketing tactic to a pivotal part of any contemporary marketing strategy. However, businesses that delve into social media marketing often encounter mile-high roadblocks that can hamper growth and success (Dutta, 2020). This article illuminates some common challenges practitioners face in social media marketing and offers strategies on how to surmount them.

1. Keeping up with changes: Social media platforms are notorious for continuously altering their algorithms, interface designs, and policies. This necessitates marketers to be agile and updated. A solid strategy to combat this challenge is by maintaining an ongoing commitment to learning and experimenting, attending webinars and workshops, and consulting relevant blogs and publications.

2. Content saturation: Due to the proliferation of content available online, it's becoming harder for businesses to capture and hold attention. To rise above the persistent noise, businesses should strategically focus on unique, engaging content that adds clear value to their audience. This could involve employing visual storytelling, addressing timely issues, or offering a fresh perspective on common topics.

3. Demonstrating ROI: Often, businesses struggle to measure and demonstrate the return on investment (ROI) for social media campaigns. Adopting advanced analytics tools and formulating a strategic social media measurement plan can be effective at showcasing the links between social media activities and concrete business outcomes (Patterson, 2018).

4. Engagement: It's not sufficient to just be present on social media; businesses need to interact with their audience. Effective engagement strategies include prompt responses to queries and comments, personalizing responses to foster connection, and posing questions or offering incentives to stimulate interaction.

These obstacles, while prominent, are surmountable with the right strategies. Embrace the ever-changing nature of social media, stand out with unique content, communicate ROI effectively, and foster authentic engagement to conquer the social media marketing sphere. Further exploration into these issues will undoubtedly yield more effective ways to navigate the treacherous yet exciting waters of social media marketing.

Legal Aspects of Social Media Marketing

In today's digitally powered world, social media has emerged as an effective and engaging marketing tool. Businesses now connect with consumers on platforms like Facebook, Instagram, Twitter, and LinkedIn. However, it is important to understand the legal aspects associated with social media marketing to avoid any elements that might violate the rules and regulations. This article outlines key legal issues about social media marketing practices.

Firstly, copyright infringement is a major issue. Posts, images, videos, or any content shared on social media must be original or should have the consent of the rightful owner. Sharing copyrighted materials without requisite permissions could lead to legal disputes and penalties (Ko, 2021).

Secondly, the Federal Trade Commission (FTC) has guidelines regarding endorsements and testimonials in advertising, which also apply to social media marketing. For instance, if an influencer is promoting a product, they must disclose if they are sponsored, being paid, or received the product for free (Federal Trade Commission, 2017).

Another issue pertains to privacy and data protection. With the advent of General Data Protection Regulations (GDPR) in Europe and similar laws worldwide, organizations need to be cautious about how they collect, store, use, and disclose personal data (Hopkins & Zweig,

2018). Non-compliance could lead to severe legal consequences including hefty fines.

Businesses also need to closely monitor user-generated content on their social platforms because they can be held accountable for any unlawful or defamatory content. Monitoring can be complicated, as too much moderation might infringe upon freedom of speech rights (Ko, 2021).

Lastly, false advertising or misleading claims can attract legal disputes. Under FTC regulations, all advertising claims must be substantiated and not misleading. Some businesses may exaggerate the benefits of their products or services on social platforms, leading to potential legal actions (Federal Trade Commission, 2017).

In conclusion, while social media marketing offers an array of opportunities for businesses, it is crucial to understand and adhere to legal requirements. By respecting copyright laws, disclosing paid promotions, protecting user data, monitoring user-generated content, and avoiding false claims, businesses can leverage the power of social media while mitigating potential legal risks.

Conclusion

Recap of Key Points Covered

Social media marketing has emerged as a critical instrument in the modern marketing toolkit. It is a dynamic and rapidly evolving field that harnesses the power of social media platforms to engage with consumers, build brands, and drive sales (Neill, 2015)[1]. This article aims to recap key points covered in the realm of social media marketing.

The primary purpose of social media marketing is boosting visibility and improving brand engagement. Companies leverage various social media platforms to communicate their messages, promote their products or services, and facilitate interactions with their target audience (Ngai, Tao & Moon, 2015)[2]. They devise strategic campaigns aimed at creating and sharing content that resonates with consumers, engender trust, and foster long-term connections.

An essential component of this marketing strategy is the selection and optimal use of suitable social media platforms. Each platform - be it Facebook, Instagram, Twitter, or LinkedIn - caters to specific audience demographics and possesses unique aspects that make them more apt for certain types of content than others (Bright, Kleiser & Grau, 2015)[3]. Thus, marketers need to strategically select and manage these platforms to suit their marketing objectives.

Content is the centerpiece of social media marketing. From beautifully curated photos, engaging videos, and compelling text posts to interactive polls and quizzes, marketers utilize a variety of content formats to engage with their audience. Moreover, elements of Content Marketing - producing valuable, relevant, consistent content - are entrenched in social media marketing (Pulizzi, 2012)[4].

A close cousin to content creation is content curation. This involves gathering, selecting, and sharing high-quality, relevant content developed by others. By curating content, marketers can provide varied, valuable information to their followers, reducing resource constraints and boosting credibility (Halligan & Shah, 2014)[5].

A crucial facet of successful social media marketing is the effective use of analytics and metrics. Tools like Google Analytics, Facebook Insights, and Instagram Analytics provide invaluable data on user engagement, reach, demographics, and other statistics. Insight from such tools helps marketers evaluate the success of their strategies and make data-driven decisions for future campaigns (De Vries, Gensler & Leeflang, 2017)[6].

Last, but not least, social media marketing heavily relies on building and maintaining relationships with the audience. This extends beyond mere 'likes' or 'follows' - the key lies in generating interactive, meaningful conversations that enlighten, engage, and entertain (Hoffman & Fodor, 2010)[7].

In conclusion, Social Media Marketing encapsulates a broad and complex range of practices, pivoting on the use of digital platforms to foster relationships, build reputation, and influence consumer behavior. With the continuous progress of digital technology and changing trends in consumer behavior, it is a domain that will continue to evolve and grow.

Importance of Keeping Up With Social Media Marketing Trends

In this digital age, social media marketing is an essential component of business strategy. Contemporary enterprises have to harness the power of social media and customize their marketing techniques in line with emerging trends. With a global user base of more than 3.6 billion people, social media platforms provide businesses with an unprecedented consumer outreach capability (Clement, 2020). Keeping up with social media marketing trends is vital for businesses to remain competitive, and increase brand visibility, and consumer engagement, therefore bolstering profitability.

A critical aspect of staying updated with social media trends is the appreciation of the dynamic nature of these platforms. A success strategy in the present context may not necessarily translate into success in the future, implying the need for businesses to keep evolving. Major social media platforms like Instagram, Twitter, and Facebook frequently update their features, necessitating that businesses adjust their marketing strategies to leverage these new tools effectively.

Moreover, understanding the current trends allows businesses to tap into consumer behavior and preferences. For instance, Facebook Insights and Instagram Analytics track user engagement, giving invaluable insights into what content resonates the most with audiences (Zephoria Digital Marketing, 2020). This information can be used to tweak marketing strategies to cater more effectively to the target audience.

The rise and subsequent ubiquity of influencers on social media platforms is another trend that businesses should not overlook. Influencer marketing is a powerful tool that can substantially increase brand visibility and credibility given that consumers tend to trust recommendations from individuals they can relate to more than conventional advertisements (Markerly, 2018).

Live videos and stories, a trend popularized largely by Instagram but now adopted by other platforms like Facebook and LinkedIn, provide another medium for businesses to interact more directly and authentically with their audiences. Businesses can leverage these tools to deliver real-time updates, behind-the-scenes content, or live Q&A sessions, adding a personalized touch to their social media engagement (Sprout Social, 2018).

Finally, it's vital to understand that social media is more than just a promotional tool, it's also an essential platform for customers to communicate with businesses. Social customer service, a trend embraced by contemporary businesses, enables companies to resolve issues or queries in real-time and provide a more satisfying customer experience (Kumar and Mirchandani, 2012).

In conclusion, to thrive in the digital marketplace, businesses must regularly update and adapt their strategies in line with social media marketing trends. By doing this, they can maintain a dynamic and effective presence on social media platforms, ensuring sustainable competitiveness, customer loyalty, and profitability.

Resources

Recommended Social Media Marketing Tools

The advent of social media has unequivocally changed the face of marketing, thereby necessitating the use of sophisticated tools that can boost your social media marketing campaign's effectiveness. These tools not only assist in content management and audience engagement but also provide useful analytical insights that can help optimize your social media strategy. This article will recommend five of the most robust social media marketing tools used by businesses worldwide.

Hootsuite is arguably one of the most popular social media marketing tools in the market today. It allows users to manage multiple social media platforms from a single dashboard, saving a considerable amount of time and effort. Hootsuite also provides in-depth analytics reports, enabling businesses to assess their performance across multiple channels efficiently(1).

Buffer is another user-friendly platform that allows users to schedule posts for various social media platforms. An intuitive interface, coupled with the ability to analyze post-performance, makes Buffer an excellent tool for maintaining consistent engagement with your audience(2).

Sprout Social's suite of social media management tools is geared towards businesses growing their brand presence across different social media outlets. It boasts comprehensive publishing, engagement, and analytics tools that streamline the process of managing and understanding social media efforts(3).

Canva is a fantastic tool for creating visually compelling social media content. With a vast library of design templates suited for different social media platforms, Canva is a real asset for those who want to add a touch of creativity to their social media campaign without the need for graphic design expertise(4).

Lastly, Buzzsumo is an excellent tool for content marketing and SEO. It allows users to search for the most shared or 'buzzing' content online, providing valuable insights into current trends. Buzzumo also comes in handy when planning content strategies, as it gives an idea about the kind of content that generates attention and shares(5).

Choosing the right social media marketing tool can be a game-changer for your business's online presence. Considerations should include your business needs, the features offered by the tool, ease of use, and, most importantly, whether it aligns with your overall social media strategy. Each of these tools offers unique features and benefits, providing ample opportunities for businesses to engage their audience, manage content, and track their online performance.

In conclusion, social media marketing tools such as Hootsuite, Buffer, Sprout Social, Canva, and Buzzsumo offer diverse solutions aimed at improving your social media presence. These tools not only enhance content delivery but also provide crucial insights into audience engagement and content performance. Ultimately, the success of your social media strategy will heavily depend on choosing and effectively utilizing the right tool for your business.

Books and Journals on Social Media Marketing

Social media marketing, an integral part of digital marketing in contemporary times, fascinates many with a keen interest in the marketing field. The vast sphere of social media marketing includes various imperative aspects, such as content creation, audience targeting, branding, and collaboration. Hence, a multitude of books and scholarly journals on social media marketing are available to appeal to different learners' needs.

Books serve as a comprehensive source of information and knowledge, creating a foundational understanding of social media marketing. Among many, "Likeable Social Media" by Dave Kerpen stands out for its in-depth discussion on how to create a brand that consumers find attractive and reliable (Kerpen, 2019). Furthermore, Shama Hyder's "The Zen of Social Media Marketing" provides practical insight into the world of online marketing. It not only teaches about the use of different social media platforms but also outlines strategies for gaining maximum engagement (Hyder, 2016).

Academic journals, on the other hand, offer well-researched, peer-reviewed information. They focus on specific topics within the larger domain of social media marketing and keep readers updated with current trends, case studies, and theories. The "Journal of Interactive Marketing" is one such resource that presents articles focusing on contemporary interactive marketing paradigms, aiding businesses to develop effective strategies (JIM, n.d.). Another renowned source is the "International Journal of Information Management." This journal publishes articles on various aspects of digital information management, including social media marketing, that assist in understanding the intricacies of the field and the strategies to be adopted for successful outcomes (IJIM, n.d.).

There are numerous books and journals dedicated to social media marketing, each providing a unique perspective on the subject. Learning through these resources not only aids in understanding the complexities of social media marketing but also helps learners to stay updated with the ever-evolving marketing trends. Therefore, professionals and students in the field of marketing need to explore various informational resources, be it books or academic journals, to enrich their understanding and skills in social media marketing.

1. Dave Kerpen. (2019). "Likeable Social Media: How to Delight Your Customers, Create an Irresistible Brand, and Be Generally Amazing on All Social Networks That Matter." McGraw Hill Education.

2. Shama Hyder. (2016). "The Zen of Social Media Marketing: An Easier Way to Build Credibility, Generate Buzz, and Increase Revenue." Benbella Books.

3. Journal of Interactive Marketing, (n.d.). Elsevier. https://www.journals.elsevier.com/journal-of-interactive-marketing

4. International Journal of Information Management, (n.d.). Elsevier. https://www.journals.elsevier.com/international-journal-of-information-management In-text

Online courses and Webinars for Further Learning

Social media is an unavoidable tool in today's business world. Its strategic incorporation into marketing strategies has made it an essential professional skill. To acquire proficiency in social media marketing, there are numerous online courses and webinars designed to equip those interested with the necessary skills. They offer further learning for marketing professionals, individual brands, and businesses to expand their reach, increase engagement, and convert followers into potential customers.

These online learning platforms provide an avenue to understand the nitty-gritty of social media networks, content creation, digital advertising, and audience engagement. Among the numerous available options, platforms like edX and Coursera offer courses specializing in social media management, empowering learners with comprehensive tools to enhance consumer interactions through robust social media campaigns (1)(2).

The online course "Social Media Marketing" by Northwestern University on Coursera delves into how to develop a deep understanding of social media tools, techniques, and strategies (2). Simultaneously, "Social Media Management" by the Boston University on edX teaches learners how to develop, implement, and assess a comprehensive digital marketing strategy (1).

Facebook Blueprint is another commendable learning program that offers all-inclusive training for advertising on Facebook and Instagram. It provides industry-specific knowledge for marketing professionals to enhance their social media marketing campaigns on these platforms (3).

Webinars have also gained traction as powerful online learning tools. They offer interactive sessions on topics related to social media marketing. Unbounce's monthly webinar series "The Landing Page Sessions" takes a comprehensive look at digital advertising and lead generation strategies, email marketing, and social media marketing. Social Media Today's live webinars offer insights into the latest trends and best practices, with guest speakers being some of the industry's most respected experts (4)(5).

Social Media Marketing Society provides access to an archive of webinars aimed at understanding social media algorithms and improving organic reach and engagement (6). Such webinars often touch upon elements of content strategy, audience targeting, and performance analytics, allowing learners to engage with experts.

Amid the confluence of technology and marketing, it is vital to ensure continuous learning in social media marketing. The rich resources offered by online courses and webinars can be instrumental in upgrading skills and staying competitive in an increasingly digitized business landscape.

Appendix

VIII. Legal Aspects of Social Media Marketing

IX. Conclusion

    A. Recap of Key Points Covered

    B. Importance of Keeping Up With Social Media Marketing Trends

X. Resources

    A. Recommended Social Media Marketing Tools

    B. Books and Journals on Social Media Marketing

    C. Online courses and Webinars for Further Learning